# The Big Sewing Book
# Little Gifts

# The Big Sewing Book
# Little Gifts

Rabea Rauer and Yvonne Reidelbach

# Before you start

## Working with the pattern sheets

There are two pages of pattern sheets, A and B. To help you find the pattern quickly, the letter of the sheet is shown by each design.

All the parts of a pattern that belong together are laid out in the same colour, so you can quickly distinguish them from pieces of other patterns in different colours. Almost all the patterns are full-size and do not need to be enlarged on a copier. A few of the patterns are not full-scale, in which case the respective dimensions are shown in centimeters. Using a tape measure, convert the pattern pieces to the measurements provided. Where necessary, the seam allowances are already included.

Place the pattern-cutting paper under the pattern sheet. Place dressmaker's carbon paper in between, with the coated side down. Now go round all the outlines of a pattern piece in one colour with a tracing wheel or a pencil. Transfer the markings inside as well, such as darts, grain of fabric, direction of nap and fold lines. When copying the different pieces, take care always to move the pattern paper just far enough so that the individual pieces lie side by side on the paper and do not overlap. Cut each pattern piece out of the pattern-cutting paper along the outer lines. Then write on the paper the name of the pattern piece and the number of times it must be cut out of the fabric and/or fusible interfacing. If appropriate, mark the edges that must be placed on a fold. Prepare all the pieces of the pattern in this way.

## What is ...

**... the degree of difficulty?**    There are little gift boxes by each design denoting the degree of difficulty. One gift box means "easy": these articles are relatively quick to make, even for beginners. Patterns marked with two gift boxes are moderately difficult. You should only try the designs with three gift boxes if you have some experience and patience, as they require more time and effort.

**... this arrow → on the pattern?**    This arrow on the pattern piece shows the straight grain or the direction of the nap of the fabric.

# Contents

# Foreword

How nice to give someone special a little present – especially when the gift is something you have made yourself. So why not have a go and show how much you care? With a few pieces of leftover fabric and coloured threads, you and your sewing machine can create charming gifts to grace the home, useful little bags, attractive pendants and fashionable accessories.

Surprise your best friend with a colourful purse, an attractive scarf or a charming brooch whilst IT enthusiasts will love the gift of an original camera case or a tablet holder! You could even present someone with a lovely memento of a joint holiday in the form of a photo displayed in a homemade frame and stressed friends will never again want to be parted from their cat-shaped neck cushion, filled with cherry stones! It is also a safe bet that your four-legged friends and their owners will absolutely love your gift of a new dog cushion.

There is no need to wait for a special occasion to bring pleasure to someone special. Sit down at your sewing machine today and simply get started. The full-size patterns provided and the precise step-by-step instructions will guarantee that your gifts will turn out perfectly. So, double the joy of gift-giving by not only bringing pleasure to the recipient, but enjoying yourself at the same time!

Rabea Rauer and Yvonne Reidelbach

# Sewing machines

*To sew successfully you need a sewing machine that works well and selects many settings automatically. This is especially helpful for beginners with no experience to rely on, but also makes life considerably easier for more advanced sewers.*

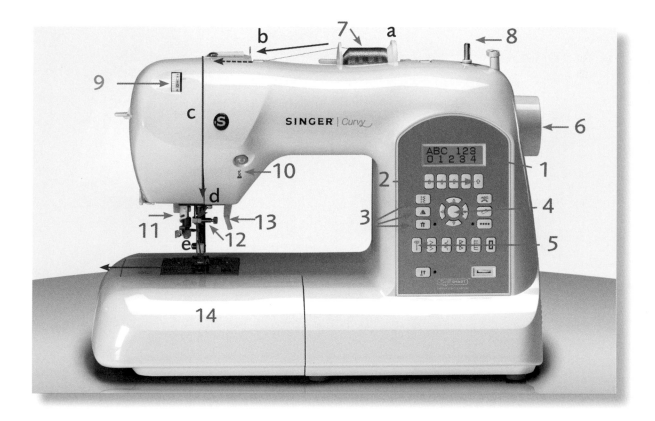

The basic requirements for a new sewing machine are that it should be very easy to handle and operate. Thanks to computer technology, it offers 225 sewing programmes, seven different buttonholes and a wide range of stitches, making it attractive even for those who only have a small budget available.

It is easy to select stitches using the selector buttons. Infinitely variable stitch width and length can be set – even while sewing – using sliders.

Modern sewing machines may also have an automatic threader, a quick-start spool and automatic tension adjustment – which are a great advantage for beginners.

The removable extension table, in which various accessories such as additional presser feet, bobbins etc. can be kept handy, makes it easy to manoeuvre items like sleeves and trouser legs under the foot.

## Controls and their functions

*1* LCD display, shows the stitch data.

*2* Multi-function keys, for selecting patterns setting the stitch width and length etc. or confirming changes to settings or returning to previous settings.

*3* Keys for utility stitches, mirror-image patterns and twin needles.

*4* Arrow and cursor keys, for moving the display of pattern groups, single patterns and the cursor.

*5* Direct selection keys for selecting stitch-patterns.

*6* Hand wheel, allows you to sew single stitches by turning the wheel with your hand.

*7* Horizontal thread guide.

*8* Bobbin winder spool pin.

*9* Upper thread tension dial.

*10* Reverse key: while the key is held down, the machine will sew the selected stitch in reverse.

*11* Automatic needle-threader makes threading up easier.

*12* At the back is a switch you press to release the presser foot.

*13* Lever for lowering/raising the presser foot at the start/end of every seam.

*14* The extension table keeps your sewing accessories handy. The lower-thread bobbin is inserted behind it.

## Threading the upper thread

*a* Place the spool of thread on the horizontal spool pin.

*b* Draw the thread from back to front over the pre-tension control.

*c* Draw the thread on down the left-hand side over the thread tensioner and down the front.

*d* Draw the thread downwards to the thread guide above the needle.

*e* Thread the yarn through the eye of the needle and pull to the left under the presser foot.

## Threading the lower thread

To wind the bobbin, place the spool of thread on the spool pin (8). Draw the thread through the thread-guide (7) to the bobbin-winder, wind round the bobbin a few times and press the button to the right of the spool. Now depress the foot pedal and the thread will be wound automatically on the bobbin. Raise the needle to its highest position using the hand wheel and open the bobbin cover. Place the bobbin in the bobbin case (turns anticlockwise), pull the thread through the front slit, then back and to the left and along the groove on the stitch plate.

# Bags and practical accessories

# Clutch purse

Size: 14 cm x 18 cm  •  Difficulty

*This pretty clutch purse is the perfect accessory for relaxed Sunday strolls or an evening out with friends. Ideal for holding coins and banknotes, as well as your handkerchief and house keys.*

**You will need:** Pattern sheet A

- cotton fabric, featuring a colourful print on beige background, 50 cm wide, 20 cm long
- iron-on interfacing, medium weight, 50 cm wide, 20 cm long
- lining of your choice, 50 cm wide, 20 cm long
- 1 plastic turquoise zip, 18 cm long
- matching thread

## Assembly instructions

**Cutting out:**
from cotton fabric: 2 x purse sections, incl. 1 cm seam allowance;

from iron-on interfacing: 2 x purse sections, incl. 1 cm seam allowance;

from the lining: 2 x purse sections, incl. 1 cm seam allowance

*1* Before cutting out, reinforce all the beige cotton fabric with iron-on interfacing. According to the pattern markings, sew the zip to the upper edges of the purse. Then, with right sides together, sew up the purse all the way round.

*2* Next, lay the purse lining pieces one on top of the other, right sides together, and sew all round the edges, leaving a small opening for turning the material right side out. Leave the upper edges open between the zip markings.

*3* With right sides together, attach the lining to the zipper seam allowance. Finally, turn the purse right side out, pushing the material through the opening in the lining, then close up the gap with a few hand stitches.

# Cosmetic bag

Size: 26 cm x 20 cm  •  Difficulty

*Ideal for taking to the office or on a weekend trip, this delightful little cosmetic bag is perfect for holding your mascara, makeup and other cosmetic essentials. This accessory also makes an idea gift for a close friend.*

**You will need:** Pattern sheet A

- cotton fabric, floral print on violet background, 1 m wide, 20 cm long
- violet and white polka-dot cotton fabric, 50 cm wide, 20 cm long
- iron-on interfacing, medium weight, 90 cm wide, 40 cm long
- lining of choice, 1 m wide, 20 cm long
- fuchsia-pink velvet ribbon, 1.3 cm wide, 50 cm long
- 1 fuchsia-pink plastic zip, 20 cm long
- matching thread

## Assembly instructions

**Cutting out:**
from the cotton print fabric: 2 x bag sections, cut on the fold, incl. 1 cm seam allowance;

from the polka-dot fabric: 4 x top panel sections, incl. 1 cm seam allowance;

from iron-on interfacing, 2 x bag sections cut on the fold, incl. 1 cm seam allowance;

from the lining: 2 x bag sections, cut on the fold, incl. 1 cm seam allowance

*1* Sew the cotton fabrics and lining separately to begin with. First reinforce the cotton fabric pieces with iron-on interfacing. Following the pattern markings, gather the folds on all the bag sections and baste in position close to the edge. Then, with right sides together, place a panel strip along the top edge of each bag section and sew together.

*2* Edge-stitch the velvet ribbon around the bag, covering the join between the panel strip and bag.

*3* Sew the zip to the top edges of the panel sections of the outer bag, then, with right sides together, sew all the way round to close up the bag.

*4* Next, with the panel strips already sewn onto the bag sections, place the lining pieces one on top of the other, right sides facing, and sew together, leaving a small opening.

*5* With right sides together, sew the lining compartment to the zip seam allowance in the cotton fabric along the zip. Then, turn the bag right side out, pushing the fabric through the opening in the lining. Close up with a few hand stitches.

**You will need:** Pattern sheet B

Size: 7 cm x 12 cm (You can adjust the pattern size to fit your smartphone or mobile phone.)

- fleece, knitted fabric, 40 cm wide, 30 cm long
- white and pink polka-dot cotton fabric, 20 cm wide, 30 cm long
- iron-on volume fleece, medium weight, 10 cm wide, 30 cm long
- 1 white mother-of-pearl button, 8 mm diameter
- 1 rhinestone, to sew on, 8 mm diameter
- matching thread

# Smartphone case

Size: 7 cm x 12 cm  •  Difficulty

*From now on, your smartphone will not only be safely cushioned against knocks and scratches but will also be contained in a neat, business-like case. You could also make the case in blue or grey fabrics and finish it off with a pointed white collar to create an alternative design suitable for a man.*

## Assembly instructions

### Cutting out:

(*Tip*: the pattern template provided is for a phone measuring 6 cm x 11.5 cm. The pattern pieces are slightly larger than the actual device so as to allow enough room to slide the phone in and out. If your smartphone/mobile is larger or smaller than the dimensions given, the difference can be added or subtracted in equal measure to or from the two sides or the length, respectively. The cuff can also be shortened or lengthened accordingly.)

from knitted fabric: 1 x sleeveless pullover front, 1 x sleeveless pullover back, 1 x cuff, inc . 7 mm seam allowance;

from cotton fabric: 2 x blouse sections, 2 x collars, incl. 7 mm seam allowance from volume fleece: 1 x blouse section

*1* Sandwich the two collar sections together with right sides facing and stitch very close to the edge along the outside. Turn right side out and press flat.

*2* Reinforce one of the blouse sections with volume fleece on the wrong side of the fabric. Then, following the pattern template, cut out the neck from both blouse pieces. Next, sandwich the two blouse sections with right sides together and insert the collar into the neckline between the two layers of fabric. The centre of the collar should be aligned with the pattern marking. Sew around the neckline, leaving a distance of 5 mm from the outside edge. Make tiny incisions into the seam allowance around the neckline curve, then tuck one blouse section to the inside through the neck opening.

*3* Close up the shoulder seams of the pullover. Fold the edge of the pullover neckline to the inside and pin to the blouse, then turn the pullover upwards and stitch around the neck edge with invisible stitches.

*4* Sandwich all layers, right sides together, and close up the side seams using a zigzag stitch or an overlock machine. Turn the smartphone case the right way out.

*5* Sew the short ends of the cuff section together, then fold the band in half lengthwise down the middle with the seam on the inside. Next, with right sides together, join the cuff to the lower edge of the case, using a zigzag stitch or overlock machine. The band should be slightly stretched as it is sewn on.

*6* Following the pattern markings, hand-sew the button and rhinestone into their respective positions on the blouse and pullover.

# Digital camera case

Size: 7 cm x 10 cm x 4 cm  •  Difficulty

*This original case, designed to resemble a camera, will keep your photo equipment safe. It includes a practical short wrist strap for secure carrying. From now on, you can be ready to take the next snapshot at all times.*

**You will need:** Pattern sheet B

- light-grey felt, 50 cm wide, 20 cm long, 3 mm thick
- black felt, 5 cm wide, 5 cm long, 1 mm thick
- white felt, 5 cm wide, 5 cm long, 1 mm thick
- red felt, 2 cm wide, 2 cm long, 1 mm thick
- corded, brightly striped ribbon, 1 cm wide, 30 cm long
- 1 light-grey, plastic zip, 33 cm long
- matching thread

## Assembly instructions

### Cutting out:

(*Tip*: the pattern provided is suitable for a digital camera measuring 6 cm x 10 cm x 3 cm. The template is slightly larger than the actual camera to allow adequate room for removing and returning the camera to its case. If your camera is larger or smaller than the dimensions given, you can always create your own pattern pieces by enlarging or reducing the pattern size.)

from light-grey felt: 1 x top part of camera case, cut on the fold, 1 x bottom part of case, cut on the fold, 2 x bases/lids, incl. 1 cm seam allowance;

from black felt: 1 x outer lens, without seam allowance;

from white felt: 1 x inner lens, 1 x flash window, without seam allowance;

from red felt: 1 x shutter release button  without seam allowance

*1* Using a buttonhole stitch, appliqué the white lens to the centre of the black lens. Following the pattern markings, sew the lenses, plus flash and shutter button, onto the light-grey felt, again using a buttonhole stitch.

*2* Sew the zip to the long sides of the top and lower sections of the case, noting the pattern markings for where the zip begins and ends.

*3* Fold the corded ribbon in half in the middle and place in position as shown on the pattern – with the loop lying on the felt. Sew up the case along the short side. Trim back the seam allowance and top-stitch along the outer edges.

*4* Next, sew the top and base to the upper and lower edges of the case, respectively, making absolutely sure that you leave a seam allowance of exactly 1 cm. Make generous incisions in the corners (without cutting into the seam!). Trim back the seam allowance as far as possible.

*5* Turn the camera case right way out and press the seams open, one at a time, using a sleeve ironing board, so that they lie nice and flat.

19

# Tablet holder

Size: according to tablet size · Difficulty

*This colourful holder will help keep your tablet safe. It is well padded and can be taken anywhere. The soft cover is equally suitable for a laptop. All you have to do is adjust the size to fit your equipment.*

**You will need:** Pattern sheet A

- 1 to 2 squares of pink felt (depending on tablet size), A3, 3 mm thick
- pink-and-red striped cotton fabric (lining), 1.40 m wide, 60 cm long
- 1 black button, 4 cm diameter
- black silk cord, 25 cm long, 2 mm thick
- matching thread

## Assembly instructions

**Cutting out:**
from the felt: 1 x front section, 1 x back section with flap, 1 x side piece, incl. seam allowance;
from the lining: 1 x front section, 1 x back section with flap, 1 x side piece, incl. 1 cm seam allowance

*1* Pin the felt side piece to the sides and base of the front section, then sew together. Repeat the procedure with the back section, including the flap, leaving an opening of 1 cm at the start and finish of the seam. (This is necessary when it comes to sewing the cotton fabric to the felt later on.) Make a generous cut into the corners and trim back the seam allowances a little. Carefully turn the case right side out.

*2* Carry out the same procedure with the lining but leaving a gap of approx. 10 cm for turning.

*3* Pin the silk cord to the flap at the spot shown on the pattern marking. With right sides together, pin the cotton flap to the felt flap, with the cord between the two layers. Sew all the way around.

*4* With right sides together, pin the front and side sections of lining to the felt front and side pieces, then sew all the way around the edge.

*5* Turn the lining compartment right side out through the opening, then close up with a few hand stitches.

*6* Press the felt seam allowances flat using a steam iron. If so desired, top-stitch around the edge of the flap, keeping close to the edge. Finally sew on the button in the positioned marked on the pattern.

# Book cover with bookmark

Size: 13,5 x 19 x 4 cm  •  Difficulty

*A special book cover is an original way to gift wrap books and will lend a personal touch to a present for a bookworm. The cover and elastic band will also protect the book from marks and dog-eared pages. The integrated bookmark will prevent you losing your place between reading sessions.*

**You will need:** Pattern sheet A

(*Tip*: The instructions given are for a paperback book, 13.5 x 19 x 4 cm)

- patchwork style cotton print, 80 cm wide, 30 cm long
- iron-on interfacing, medium thickness, 80 cm wide, 30 cm long
- violet-striped elastic band, 2.5 cm wide, 25 cm long
- blue-and-white checked ribbon, 7 mm wide, 13 cm long
- bookmark: piece of fabric cut into a butterfly or flower shape, plus interfacing (optional)
- matching thread

## Assembly instructions

**Cutting out:**
from the cotton fabric and interfacing: Width = 1 x length of the book + 4 cm seam allowance; Length = 2 x width of the book + 1 x width of the spine + 2 x 12 cm for the inside flap;

from elastic band: Length = length of the book + 2 x width of the spine, without a seam allowance so that the band fits tightly;

for the bookmark: 2 x butterfly or flower shapes (the same on both sides), just roughly cut out, to begin with

*1* Reinforce the cotton fabric with the interfacing and neaten the edges all the way around with zigzag stitch or using an overlock machine.

*2* Place the blue-and-white checked ribbon for the book mark between the front and back sections of the butterfly, sew around the shape close to the edge using a buttonhole stitch and trim around the stitching using a small pair of scissors.

*3* Following the pattern markings, fix the end of the bookmark ribbon in the middle of the long side of the fabric using zigzag stitches and keeping as close as possible to the edge.

*4* With right sides together and 14 cm away from the edge (cf. pattern marking), sew one end of the elastic band to the top of the fabric and the other end to the lower section, using zigzag stitches. The elasticated band should be tightly stretched and under tension.

*5* Next, fold over and press each of the short sides of fabric 2 cm in. Then make another crease 10 cm in and press flat. Next, fold back the fabric along the second crease so that the fabric is lying right sides together. Finally, leaving a seam allowance of 2 cm, sew along the edge of the cover flap, turn right side out and press.

# Penguin pendant

Size: 4 cm x 9 cm • Difficulty

*A delightful gift for people who are always losing their keys. This cute little penguin is guaranteed to make lost keys and tiresome searches a thing of the past. The pendant could also double as a lucky charm.*

## You will need: Pattern sheet A

- dark-blue cotton fabric with white polka dots, 20 cm wide, 15 cm long
- white cotton fabric with pink polka dots, 10 cm wide, 15 cm long
- iron-on interfacing, medium thickness, 30 cm wide, 15 cm long
- yellow felt, 5 cm wide, 3 cm long, 1 mm thick
- black felt, 3 cm wide, 3 cm long, 1 mm thick
- fibre filling
- textile adhesive
- silver key ring, approx. 5 cm long
- tear-resistant ribbon in dark blue (for the key ring), approx. 6 cm long
- matching thread

## Assembly instructions

**Cutting out:**

from dark blue cotton fabric: 2 x body sections, incl. 5 mm seam allowance;

from white cotton fabric: 1 x front, no seam allowance;

from the interfacing: 2 x body sections, incl. 5 mm seam allowance, 1 x front, no seam allowance;

from yellow felt: 1 x beak, 2 x feet;

from black felt: 2 x eyes

*1* Reinforce the body sections and white tummy section on the wrong side with interfacing. Pin the white front to one of the body sections and sew around the edge using a buttonhole stitch.

*2* Position and pin the feet to the body section, according to the marks on the pattern, toes pointing forward. Fold the ribbon for the key ring in half and pin it onto the head, the loop should point to the middle of the body.

*3* With right sides together, pin one body section to the other and sew the layers together all the round the edge, leaving a gap of approx. 3 cm on one wing, according to the pattern markings. Carefully turn the penguin right way out through this opening.

*4* Stuff the penguin with wadding and carefully close up the opening with invisible hand stitches. Stick on the eyes and beak with fabric adhesive. Finally, attach the pendant to a link on the key ring with the aid of pliers.

# Cupcake pin cushion

Size: 14 cm high, 14 cm diameter  •  Difficulty

*From now on, your sewing needles, pins and safety pins will have a very special place of their own. This cute pin cushion will delight any sewing enthusiast. And there will be no need to diet afterwards!*

**You will need:** Pattern sheet A

- pink, floral print cotton fabric, 30 cm wide, 30 cm long
- beige cord material, 40 cm wide, 30 cm long
- iron-on interfacing, medium weight, 30 cm wide, 30 cm long
- a few rocaille pearls, sequins and sparkling stones in red and pink
- 1 apricot, raised button, 2 cm diameter
- 1 yoghurt container (circular)
- soft stuffing
- matching thread

## Assembly instructions

**Cutting out:**

(*Tip*: The pattern for the cord fabric can be shaped around the yoghurt carton.)

from cotton fabric: 1 x cake cut on the fold (N.B.: two folds; you need a whole circle!), incl.1 cm seam allowance;

from the cord material: 1 x base, 2 x sides, incl. 1 cm seam allowance;

from the interfacing: 1 x cake, cut on the fold (N.B.: two folds; you need a whole circle!), incl. 1 cm seam allowance

*1* With right sides together, sew the side seams of the cord fabric together. Again, with right sides together, sew the base to the sides all the way round, then turn the whole thing right side out. Insert the yoghurt carton.

*2* Reinforce the cotton fabric circle with interfacing. Using maximum stitch length and keeping close to the edge, stitch all around the edge of the circle, but do not fix the seam. Pull the ends of thread to gather the whole outside edge. (This thread can be removed once sewing is completed.)

*3* Fold the outer edge to the inside and pin at irregular intervals to the upper edge of the cord base, producing a wavy line to imitate the cream spilling over the edge of the cake. Fix three-quarters of the fabric in this way, then stuff with plenty of wadding. Pin the rest of the outside edge together.

*4* Sew the two fabrics together using tiny, invisible stitches, adding a little more wadding from time to time to ensure that the stuffed pin cushion is firm and bulging.

*5* Finally, decorate the cup cake, as desired, with pearls, sequins or rhinestones, stitching these on by hand. Fix the apricot-coloured button to the centre of the cake.

Pretty and practical
gift ideas for the home

# Handmade picture frame

Size: 20 cm x 24 cm • Difficulty

This fabric picture frame makes a perfect surround for displaying favourite photographs. Ideal as a gift for a favoured work colleague or a beloved grandma, this decorative gift is quick to make. You can add a magical, personal touch by using a fabric chosen to coordinate with the home décor of the person in question.

**You will need:** Pattern sheet B

(*Tip*: suitable for a photo 9 cm x 13 cm)

- blue cotton fabric with white polka dots, 25 cm wide, 25 cm long
- red-and-white gingham check fabric, 50 cm wide, 25 cm long (to cover the rear of the frame)
- iron-on interfacing, medium weight, 75 cm wide, 25 cm long
- red, decorative bobble border, 1 cm wide, 50 cm long
- red cord, 13 cm long, 4 mm thick
- matching thread
- fabric adhesive
- 4 photo corners or two-sided adhesive tape

## Assembly instructions

### Cutting out:

(*Tip*: You can make the picture frame larger or smaller, depending on the size of your photo.)

from polka-dot cotton fabric: 1 x photo frame with a window cut out along the broken line, incl.1 cm seam allowance;

from checked cotton fabric: 2 x photo frames, incl. 1 cm seam allowance;

from iron-on interfacing: 3 x photo frames, 1 to include a cut-out window

*1* Reinforce all the fabric sections on the wrong side with interfacing. On the polk-dot fabric section, cut into the corners of the window along the cutting line indicated on the pattern. Fold a 1-cm seam allowance to the inside and iron. Sew the bobble border around the window outline, keeping close to the edge.

*2* Sandwich the two pieces of checked fabric, wrong sides together, and stitch together, keeping close to the edge. This will form the back of the picture frame.

*3* Lay the 13-cm long cord for hanging the photo frame onto the right side of the checked fabric and pin in the appropriate position indicated on the pattern. Then, lay the dotted fabric on top, right sides together, and sew the layers together keeping a distance of 1 cm from the outside edge.

*4* Cut off the corners, then turn the frame inside out through the window. Stick the two layers together, using some fabric glue, and insert a photo in the centre using photo corners or two-sided adhesive tape.

# Reversible plant pot cover

Size: 20 cm high, 16 cm diameter • Difficulty

*Printed cotton fabrics can jazz up ordinary plant pots with a splash of colour in the blink of an eye. Even simple, green foliage plants can be turned into eye-catching features. A bright cover like this will lend your gift of a potted plant a special, personal touch. And if you become a little bored with one side, you can create a completely new look by turning the other way out.*

## You will need:

(*Tip*: The dimensions given are suitable for a pot approx. 19 cm high, 15 cm diameter)

- colourful print cotton fabric, 1 m wide, 40 cm long
- blue-and-white striped cotton fabric, 1 m wide, 40 cm long
- iron-on interfacing, medium thickness, 1 m wide, 40 cm long
- matching thread

## Assembly instructions

### Cutting out:

Using a pencil, measuring tape and a set square, draw the pattern onto a sheet of paper.

**Base:** Circle around the base of the plant pot, adding an extra 2 cm (1 cm clearance + 1 cm seam allowance).

**Side section:** Draw a rectangle the long side = the circumference of the base, exclusive of seam allowance (1 cm) x the short side = the height of the pot + 6 cm. Add 1 cm seam allowance all the way round the rectangle.

from cotton fabric print: 1 x base, 1 x side section, incl. 1 cm seam allowance;

from blue-and-white striped cotton fabric: 1 x base, 1 x side section, incl. 1 cm seam allowance;

from iron-on interfacing: 1 x base, 1 x side section, incl. 1 cm seam allowance

*1* Reinforce the cotton print sections with interfacing. Then, with right sides together, sew the two short ends of the print fabric side piece, and iron the seam flat. Repeat this procedure with the other side piece in striped fabric but leaving a gap of 7 cm for turning.

*2* Next, insert the two bases into the respective side sections, right sides together.

*3* Place one pot cover inside the other, then, with right sides facing, sew the two covers together along the upper edge. Turn right side out through the opening, then close using a few hand stitches. The top edge can now be folded over for contrast.

# For the breakfast table

Everyone will enjoy sitting down at this breakfast table. The crusty, breakfast rolls are displayed in this beautiful, practical basket of cotton and linen and the decorative place settings are extremely pretty and keep the table tidy. Not only do they create an attractive setting for the plates but also incorporate cutlery holders. Boiled eggs, kept warm under these charming little egg cosies, provide the perfect finishing touch to this delightful breakfast table. (Cf. P 36-39 for instructions).

**You will need:** Pattern sheet A

(*Tip*: The instructions are for two place settings.)

- plain linen, 1.40 m wide, 70 cm long
- floral print cotton fabric, 1.40 m wide, 35 cm long
- iron-on interfacing, medium thick, 90 cm wide, 1.50 m long
- matching thread

# Place mats with cutlery holders

Size: 47 cm x 32 cm and 10 cm x 26 cm • Difficulty

## Assembly instructions

### Cutting out:

(*Tip*: Cut out parallel to the selvage.)

from linen: 4 x place mats, 4 x cutlery pockets 1, incl. seam allowance;

from floral cotton print: 2 x straight side pieces, 2 x diagonal side pieces, 2 x cutlery pockets 2, incl. 1 cm seam allowance;

from the interfacing: 4 x place mats, 2 x diagonal side pieces; 4 x cutlery pockets 1, incl. 1 cm seam allowance

*1* On the wrong side, reinforce the linen place mats and cutlery pockets, as well as the diagonal side pieces in floral cotton fabric with iron-on interfacing.

*2* Fold the floral print straight side piece along the fold line shown on the pattern and pin to the left hand side of the place mat, as indicated by the pattern marking, with the folded edge towards the middle. Edge-stitch the fold to the plate mat.

*3* Similarly, fold the diagonal side piece of floral cotton print along the fold line shown on the pattern. Position and pin to the right side of the place mat, according to the markings on the pattern and position in place.

*4* Next, lay another place mat, right sides together, on the prepared place mat and sew together all the way round the outside edges, but leaving an opening 10 cm long. Cut back the corners, then turn the place mat right side out through the opening.

*5* Close up the opening with a few invisible hand stitches, press the place mat flat and top stitch all around 2 cm from the edge.

*6* Fold the cutlery holder 2 along the fabric fold and baste it to one cutlery pocket 1. Place a second cutlery holder 1, right sides together, on top of the first and sew all around the outside edges, leaving an opening approx. 8 cm long. Cut back the corners and turn the cutlery holder right way out through the gap. Close up the opening invisibly with a few hand stitches.

# Bread basket

Size: 26 cm x 26 cm   •   Difficulty

**You will need:** Pattern sheet A

- natural coloured linen, 1.20 m wide, 35 cm long
- green-and-white checked cotton fabric, 1.20 m wide, 35 cm long
- iron-on interfacing, medium weight, 90 cm wide, 80 cm long
- iron-on volume fleece, 90 cm wide, 80 cm long
- matching thread

## Assembly instructions

**Cutting out:**

from linen: 2 x sides cut on fabric fold, 1 x base cut on the fold, incl. 1 cm seam allowance;

from cotton fabric: 2 x sides cut on the fold, 1 x base cut on the fold, incl. 1 cm seam allowance;

from iron-on interfacing: 2 x sides cut on fold, 1 x base cut on fold, incl. 1 cm seam allowance;

from volume fleece: 2 x sides cut on the fold, 1 x base cut on the fold, incl. 1 cm seam allowance

*1* On the wrong side of the fabric, reinforce the linen side pieces and base with interfacing and volume fleece. Then, lay the side pieces, right sides together, on top of each other and sew the sides together.

*2* Next, with right sides together, pin the sides to the linen base, making sure that the side seams are lined up with the markings on the base as shown on the pattern. Then sew all the way round.

*3* Repeat this procedure with the checked fabric but leave an approx. 7- cm long opening on one of the side seams.

*4* Turn the linen bread basket right side out, then place the cotton fabric basket inside the linen one so that the open edges are aligned with each other, right sides together. Stitch the materials together all the way round.

*5* Turn the bread basket right way out through the opening in the checked fabric and close with a few hand stitches. Fold the upper edge over to show a band of green-and-white checked fabric. The bread basket can be reversed, if desired.

# Egg warmers

Size: 6 cm x 7 cm  •  Difficulty

**You will need:** Pattern sheet A

(*Tip*: makes 4 egg warmers)

- green and white polka-dot cotton fabric, 1 m wide, 25 cm long
- iron-on volume fleece, 50 cm wide, 25 cm long
- red- or green-checked ribbon, 7 mm wide, 32 cm long
- floral border, 1,5 cm wide, 90 cm long
- matching thread

## Assembly instructions

### Cutting out:

from cotton fabric: 16 x egg warmers, incl. 7 mm seam allowance;

from volume fleece: 8 x egg warmers, incl. 7 mm seam allowance

*1* Reinforce eight of the egg warmer fabric pieces with volume fleece on the wrong side. The remaining eight egg warmer sections will serve as linings. Place them on top of the eight reinforced sections, right sides together, and sew them together 7 mm inside the rounded edge. Leave an opening of approx. 3 cm on each to turn it inside out.

*2* Cut the ribbon for the loops into 8 cm-lengths. Fold these in half and fix in the appropriate position on, as shown on the pattern, on each of the reinforced egg warmer sections. The loop should be placed on the right side of the fabric, pointing into the middle.

*3* Now, right sides together, sew two of the padded sections together a short distance down one side. Press the seam allowance apart and turn right side out. Cut a 22.5 cm length of ribbon and edge-stitch the ribbon lengthwise across the two parts according to the pattern markings. Sew together the dome and the second side of each egg warmer (ensuring that the loop is caught in the seam).

*4* With right sides together, pin the lining to the lower edge of the outer pocket and sew all the way round. (NB: proceed patiently and carefully, this is a bit tricky!) and turn the egg warmer inside out through the opening in the lining. Close the gap with a few hand stitches or edge-stitch by machine and push the lining inside.

## Tip:

These egg warmers are especially attractive if they are made from lots of colourful pieces of leftover fabric and different coloured border and bands!

**You will need:** Pattern sheet B

- lime green satin, 15 cm wide, 30 cm long
- star-print cotton fabric, 10 cm wide, 10 cm long
- pink-and-white polka-dot cotton fabric, 20 cm wide, 15 cm long
- lilac linen, 15 cm wide, 15 cm long
- cotton fabric, stripes and floral print, 15 cm wide, 15 cm long
- iron-on interfacing, medium weight, 50 cm wide, 20 cm long
- white lace border, 1 cm wide, 25 cm long
- pink satin ribbon, 1 cm wide, 16 cm long
- dried lavender, for the filling
- a little wadding, if so desired
- matching thread

# Lavender scent bags

Size: each approx. 11 cm long • Difficulty

*These lavender scent bags not only deter unwanted guests from visiting your wardrobe but also look very attractive hanging from a doorknob.*

## Assembly instructions

**Cutting out:**
from satin: 2 x cushions, incl. 5 mm seam allowance;
from cotton fabric with star print: 1 x perfume bottle, without seam allowance;
from polka-dot cotton fabric: 1 x perfume bottom top, without seam allowance; 1 x heart, front top section, incl. 5 mm seam allowance;
from linen: 1 x heart, front bottom section, incl. 5 mm seam allowance;
from striped cotton fabric: 1 x heart back, incl. 5 mm seam allowance;
from iron-on interfacing: 2 x cushions, incl. 5 mm seam allowance, 1 x perfume bottle lower part, without seam allowance, 1 x perfume bottle top part, without seam allowance; 1 x heart, front top, incl. 5 mm seam allowance, 1 x heart, front bottom section, incl. 5 mm seam allowance, 1 x heart back, incl. 5 mm seam allowance

*Heart:*

*1* First of all, reinforce all the fabric pieces with iron-on interfacing. Sew the "heart front top" and "heart front bottom" pieces together. Then, cut a 9-cm length from the lace ribbon and stitch it over this seam.

*2* To make the loop, fold the remaining 16 cm of lace ribbon in half in the middle and position on the right hand side of the fabric. Then, with right sides together, place the two heart sections one

on top of the other and sew all around the edge, leaving a small gap to turn the heart right way out. Fill the heart with dried lavender and some wadding, if so desired. Finally, close up the gap with a few hand stitches.

*Perfume bottle cushion:*

*1* Begin by reinforcing all the fabric pieces with interfacing. Place the piece of perfume bottle, slightly overlapping, on the satin. Sew all the way around the edge using a buttonhole stitch.

*2* To make the loop, fold the satin ribbon in half in the middle and, following the pattern markings, position on the right-hand side of the fabric.

*3* Place the two satin pieces one on top of the other, right sides together, and sew around the edge, leaving a small gap for turning. Turn the cushion right side out and fill with dried lavender and, if so desired, a little stuffing. Close up the gap with a few hand stitches.

# Tissue box covers

Size: 12 cm x 25 cm  •  Difficulty

*These covers are quick to make and will add a touch of style to your bathroom. Jazzing them up with a few little details, such as borders and bows, will give these pretty covers a personal touch, making them an ideal gift.*

**You will need:** Pattern sheet B
(*Tip*: cover is designed to fit standard cosmetic tissue boxes)

- printed cotton fabric, 90 cm wide  20 cm long
- iron-on interfacing, medium weight, 90 cm wide, 20 cm long
- 2 bows to match the colours of the fabric print
- matching velvet ribbon, 5 mm wide, 80 cm long
- matching thread

## Assembly instructions

**Cutting out:**
from cotton print: 2 x covers cut on the fold of the fabric, incl. 1 cm seam allowance;

from iron-on interfacing: 2 x covers cut on the fold of the fabric, incl. 1 cm seam allowance

*1* Reinforce the two fabric pieces with interfacing. Then, place the fabric right sides together so that they are positioned exactly on the seam line marked on the pattern. Starting from both ends, sew together the layers along this seam as far as the slit marking (cf. as shown on the pattern).

*2* Press the seam inward along the dotted line and top-stitch 7 mm from the edge. The cover will now have a slit in the middle for tissues. Decorate each end of the slit, as desired, with bows, then stitch narrow velvet ribbon along the both top-stitched lines either side of the slit.

*3* Then, join the corner edges diagonally together to make a box shape and sew together, 1 cm in from the edge. Neaten the seam using a zigzag stitch or an overlock machine.

*4* Neaten the lower edge in the same way, then fold under a 1-cm hem and top-stitch.

# Dotty the neck pillow cat

Size: 50 cm x 35 cm  •  Difficulty

*This cuddly cat fits comfortably around your neck, its warm body, filled with cherry stones, relaxes and soothes away neck pains. And the best feature about it is that it does not shed cat hairs!*

**You will need:** Pattern sheet A

- dark-blue, white-spotted cotton fabric, 50 cm wide, 60 cm long
- dark-blue fleece, 50 cm wide, 60 cm long
- 600 g cherry stones
- matching thread

## Assembly instructions

**Cutting out:**
from cotton fabric: 1 x neck cat, incl. 7 mm seam allowance;

from fleece: 1 x neck cat, incl. 7 mm seam allowance

*1* Place the two fabrics right sides together, then, leaving a seam allowance of 7 mm, sew together all around the edge. Leave an opening between the marks shown on the pattern.

*2* Cut into all curves and corners of the seam allowance to stop the material pulling and ensure that the seam is nice and smooth.

*3* Then turn the cat right side out and fill with cherry stones. Close up the opening tightly with a few hand stitches.

**Tip for warming the cushion:**
Heat in the oven for approx. 10 minutes at a maximum temperature of 130 °C. The cushion should first be wrapped in aluminium foil first to prevent the fabric from turning brown!
The cushion can also be heated in the microwave for approx. 1 minute at max. 600 Watt. Shake thoroughly after use and allow to cool completely. The microwave plate must be clean and dry to prevent the fabric from burning.

## You will need: Pattern sheet A + B

*Sofa cushions with edging*
- Light-blue and white polka-dot cotton fabric, 1 x 42 cm wide, 42 cm long; 1 x 30 cm wide, 30 cm long
- brown and white polka-dot fabric,1 x 42 cm wide, 42 cm long (with window)
- 1 light-blue zip, 40 cm long

*Sofa cushion with ruching*
- light-blue and brown checked cotton fabric, 42 cm wide, 42 cm long (2 x)
- brown and white polka-dot cotton fabric, 1,40 m wide, 10 cm long (2 x)
- 1 light-blue or brown zip, 40 cm long

*for each cushion*
- matching thread, 1 appropriately sized cushion filler

*dog cushion*
- light-blue denim material, 82 cm wide, 82 cm long
- white cotton fabric, 70 cm wide, 40 cm long
- dog print cotton fabric, 82 cm wide, 82 cm long
- iron-on interfacing, medium weight, 70 cm wide, 40 cm long
- 1 light-blue zip, 60 cm long
- matching thread
- 1 suitably sized feather cushion

# Comfy decorative cushions

Size: 40 cm x 40 cm, or 80 cm x 80 cm for the dog bed  •  Difficulty

*Whether you opt for cushions to jazz up a sofa, a dog cushion or chair cushions, choosing a fabric to match someone's home décor will give your gift a very personal touch and is bound to delight the recipient.*

## Assembly instructions

**Cutting out (dog cushion only):**
from white cotton fabric: 1 x bone
from iron-on interfacing: 1 x bone

*1* Neaten all the edges of fabric (apart from the bone) with zigzag stitch or using an overlock machine.

*2* *To make the cushion with border*: Using the pattern outline provided, cut a window out of the brown fabric. With right sides together  sew the small square of light-blue fabric to the inner edge of the brown frame. After stitching, it is important to cut into the corners of the frame to ensure that the fabric does not pull and the seam lies nice and flat.

*3* *To make the cushion with ruching*: With right sides together, sew the short ends of the long strips of fabric together. Then, fold the strips down the middle lengthwise and, using the longest stitch on your sewing machine, sew two gathering seams close together along the open edges of the strip. Next, draw up the threads to gather the strip into a length of fabric 58 cm long. Pin or baste the strip close to the edge on one side of the cushion, so that the ruching faces inward towards the centre of the cushion, with right sides together.

*4* *To make the dog cushion*: Reinforce the bone on the wrong side of the fabric with interfacing. Pin the bone to the denim fabric, then sew all around the edge using a buttonhole stitch.

*5* The zip is inserted as described below for all three cushions: With right sides together, fix the zip to the lower edge of one of the cushion pieces and sew along the groove, as close as possible to the zip teeth. Next, sew the other side of the zip to the lower edge of the second cushion piece. It is essential that the zip be left open during sewing. Then, with right sides of the two pieces together, close up the zip a little and sew all around the edge of the cushion leaving a 1-cm seam allowance. Start to sew where the zip begins and finish sewing at the other end of the zip. Turn the cushions right way out and iron.

Trendy fashion accessories

**You will need:** Pattern sheet B

*Triangular scarf*

- green, floral viscose fabric, 1.40 m wide, 1 m long
- red cotton fabric (ideally batiste), 1.40 m wide, 1 m long
- bobble border in charcoal grey, 1 cm wide, 2,50 m long
- matching thread

## Assembly instructions

**Cutting out:**
from the green viscose fabric: 1 x scarf, incl. 1 cm seam allowance;

from the red cotton fabric: 1 x scarf, incl. 1 cm seam allowance

*1* With right sides together, baste the bobble border to the edges of the viscose triangle, making sure that the bobbles face inwards, then stitch the border all the way around.

*2* With right sides together, pin the cotton fabric to the viscose triangle and sew the two layers together all the way around, leaving open a gap of approx. 10 cm. Clip back the corners, then turn the scarf right side out through the opening, carefully pushing out the corners. Finally, close up the opening with a few invisible hand stitches.

# Triangular scarf and loop scarf

Size: 1.40 m x 70 cm and 70 cm x 35 cm • Difficulty

*A scarf made from a combination of velvet and silk or viscose and fine cotton makes a very elegant gift. Both versions are so lovely to wear that you will never want to be without one or the other. Both the triangular scarf and the loop are reversible.*

## You will need:
(*Tip*: A pattern is not provided for the loop scarf. It is simply cut out according to the measurements given below.)

*Loop scarf*
- black velvet, 1.40 m wide, 40 cm long
- silk in a black, pink and beige tendril pattern, 1.40 m wide, 40 cm long
- matching thread

## Assembly instructions

*1* With right sides together, tack the long edges of the silk and velvet sections together, then sew. Turn the scarf right side out through one of the open ends.

*2* Next, with right sides together, pin the short ends of the scarf together and sew, leaving a gap of approx. 10 cm in one end. Close this gap with a few hand stitches.

# Trendy tie belt

**Size: 11 cm x 70 cm • Difficulty**

*This smart tie belt will pep up any outfit from a summer dress or maxi skirt to a casual shirt. It is fully reversible so is extremely versatile. This eye-catching accessory makes a great gift for a fashion-conscious friend!*

**You will need: Pattern sheet A**

- black print cotton fabric, 1 m wide, 15 cm long
- lilac print cotton fabric, 1 m wide, 15 cm long
- black cotton fabric, 1 m wide, 8 cm long
- iron-on interfacing, medium weight, 90 cm wide, 60 cm long
- black border strip, 1 cm wide, 2 m long
- matching thread

## Assembly instructions

**Cutting out:**
(*Tip:* the pattern corresponds to a UK size 8 (European 36). To increase by one size at a time, add an extra 2 cm parallel to each edge, in other words a total of 4 cm for each size increase.)

from black print cotton fabric: 1 x tie belt cut on the fabric fold, without a seam allowance;

from lilac print cotton fabric: 1 x tie belt cut on the fold, without a seam allowance;

from iron-on interfacing: 2 x tie belts, cut on the fold, without a seam allowance;

from black cotton fabric: 2 x 8 cm x 50 cm for the ties, incl. 1 cm seam allowance on the short ends

*1* Reinforce the tie belt pieces with interfacing on the wrong side, then pin together, wrong sides facing, and edge-stitch using a long stitch and keeping close to the edge.

*2* Fold the black ties in half down the middle lengthwise to resemble edging tape, then press flat. Next, fold the edges once more into the middle and press again. From the original 8-cm width of fabric, you should now have a width of 2 cm. Tuck in 1 cm of one open end of each ties. Then, edge-stitch the ties all the way round.

*3* With right sides together, baste the open ends of the ties onto the edge of the lilac side of the belt, as indicated by the pattern markings, ensuring that the bands lie pointing into the middle of the belt.

*4* Fit the long border strip around the edges of the belt and sew in position close to the edge.

*5* Finally, draw the ties forward over the border, fixing them in position with a few stitches.

# Cosy wrist cuffs

Size: 26 cm x 40 cm  •  Difficulty

*These trendy wrist cuffs mean you can wear shirts with three-quarter length sleeves even in the depths of winter. Not only are the cuffs wonderfully warm and soft, but a touch of lace will make them an elegant addition to any wardrobe.*

**You will need:** Pattern sheet B

• grey boiled wool material in a floral design, 90 cm wide, 40 cm long
• black cotton jersey, 90 cm wide, 40 cm long
• black cotton lace trim, 3 cm ide, 60 cm long
• matching thread

## Assembly instructions

**Cutting out:**
from the boiled wool material: 2 x cuffs, cut on the fold (mirror image, the thumb is only on one side), 2 x thumbs (mirror image), incl. 7 mm seam allowance;
from cotton jersey: 2 x cuffs, cut on the fold (mirror image, the pattern for the thumb is only on one side), 2 x thumbs (mirror image), incl. 7 mm seam allowance

*1* With right sides together, pin the thumbs, as indicated by the markings on the pattern (1 on 1, 2 on 2), to the point where they join the cuff and then sew together, leaving 7 mm open at the beginning and the end. Repeat this procedure with the cotton jersey.

*2* Pin the lace trim to the boiled wool cuff pieces, at the points indicated on the pattern, then edge-stitch along both sides.

*3* Next, fold each of the boiled wool pieces in the middle, with the right sides facing inwards. Then sew the long sides together. On the opposite long side, sew up the dart (cf. pattern). Turn the cuffs right side out.

*4* Fold the cotton jersey cuffs likewise down the middle and sew up the long edges, leaving an opening. Close the dart on the opposite long side.

*5* Fit the cotton jersey cuffs over the wool cuffs, so that the right sides are facing. Then, pin the top openings for the fingers together all the way round. Stitch together and turn the cotton jersey to the inside.

*6* Tuck in the thumb seam allowances and sew them to the turned-in jersey all the way round with a few hand stitches.

*7* Next, place the seam allowances of the lower arm openings with right sides together and pull through the opening in the fabric. Then close up the seam all the way round. Tuck the cotton jersey to the inside again and finish by closing with a few invisible hand stitches.

**You will need:** Pattern sheet B

*Version 1 (in pink and grey)*

• pink-and-white, checked cotton fabric , 20 cm x 20 cm

• pink-and-grey dotted cotton fabric, 20 cm long

• floral print cotton fabric, 20 cm wide, 20 cm long

• pink-striped cotton fabric, 7 mm wide, 30 cm long

• pink leather ribbon, 3 mm wide, 25 cm long

• 1 red button, 2 cm diameter

• 1 silver fastening pin, 3 cm wide

• matching thread

# Trendy brooches

*These wonderful fabric brooches will enhance any type of clothing. Pinned to a jacket, they will liven up a favourite friend's routine day at the office. Even an elegant party dress or simple handbag can be jazzed up with this accessory.*

**You will need:** Pattern sheet B

*Version 2 (in black and white)*
• white cotton fabric with black dots, 40 cm wide, 20 cm long
• white lace border, 20 cm wide, 20 cm long
• black and white ribbon, 7 mm wide, 30 cm long
• black silk cord, 25 cm long, 2 mm wide
• 1 mother-of-pearl button, 2 cm diameter
• 1 silver fastening pin, 3 cm wide
• matching thread

## Assembly instructions

### Cutting out:
*Version 1*

from checked material: 1 x brooch back, incl. 7 mm seam allowance;

from polka-dot material: 2 x brooch front, incl. 7 mm seam allowance;

from floral print fabric: 2 x brooch front, incl 7 mm seam allowance

*Version 2*

from polka-dot fabric: 2 x brooch back, incl. 7 mm seam allowance;

from lace trim: 4 x brooch front (with the scalloped edge as the outside edge), incl. 7 mm seam allowance

*1* With right sides together, sew the front sections of brooch (alternating colours) into a ring.

*2* Version 1: With right sides together, place the top ring onto the ring beneath and stitch together along the outer edge. Then, turn right side out, and, with the pieces slightly misaligned, iron in such a way that the fabric below peeps out.

*3* Version 2: Place the two spotted pattern pieces right sides together and sew all around the outer edge. Turn inside out and iron, then attach the lace to the ring.

*4* Fold the ring into irregular folds and pin in place. The fabric should end up overlapping in the middle, with the hole no longer visible. Next, using a large zigzag stitch, sew across the middle to fix the folds in position.

*5* Fold the ribbons into uneven lengths and fix likewise to the centre of the brooch, then sew the button on top. On the reverse side, sew the fastener pin in place with a few hand stitches.

# Sleep mask & ballerina slippers

Size of sleep mask: 8 cm x 22 cm  •  Difficulty

Size of slippers: 8 cm x 24 cm  •  Difficulty

These items will be great to take along on every trip. Thanks to these sweet ballerina shoes, cold feet will be a thing of the past and the sleep mask is bound to help avert the effects of jet lag. A chic gift for globetrotters as well as for anyone who just wants to be comfortable at home!

**Sleep mask**

**You will need:** Pattern sheet B

- Print cotton fabric, 1 m wide, 30 cm long
- iron-on interfacing, medium weight, 50 cm wide, 30 cm long
- volume fleece to iron-on, 25 wide cm wide, 30 cm long
- strip of black lace, 1.5 cm wide, 13 cm long
- elastic band, 2 cm wide, 33 cm long
- matching thread
- safety pins

## Assembly instructions

**Cutting out:**

from cotton fabric: 2 x sleep masks, 1 x tunnel strip for the elasticated band, incl. 1 cm seam allowance;

from iron-on interfacing: 2 x face masks, incl. 1 cm seam allowance;

from volume fleece: 1 x face mask

*1* Reinforce the cotton fabric face mask sections with interfacing and volume fleece. Cut the lace strip for the eyelashes into two equal lengths, fold the ends over on the inside and then sew into position according to the markings on the pattern.

*2* With right sides together, fold the tunnel strip of fabric in half lengthwise and sew the long side together. Next, using a safety pin, turn the fabric right side out, then draw the elastic through the "tunnel".

*3* Pin or tack the elasticated band to the face mask at the points indicated on the pattern. Lay the face mask pieces right sides together with the elasticated band in between. Then, sew all around the edge of the face mask, leaving open a small gap for turning the fabric right way out. Trim back the seam a little. Turn the mask right way out, press flat and close up the gap with a few hand stitches.

## Ballerina slippers (UK size 5)
**You will need:** Pattern sheet B

- pink cotton floral print, 1.40 m wide, 30 cm long
- pink fleece, 30 cm wide, 30 cm long
- grey Alcantara synthetic suede fabric, 30 cm wide, 30 cm lang
- iron-on interfacing, medium weight, 90 cm wide, 50 cm long
- fuchsia-pink velvet ribbon, 7 mm wide, 80 cm long
- elastic band, 7 mm wide, 20 cm long
- fabric adhesive
- matching thread
- small safety pin

## Assembly instructions

### Cutting out:
(*Tip*: Right and left shoe are identical. To cut fabric pieces for shoes in other sizes, proceed as follows: for smaller sizes, the fabric piece is adjusted along the sides. With Size 5 as the template, reduce each side by cutting off 1 cm per size parallel to the edge of the folded piece. To make larger sizes, add an appropriate amount of extra length. To make the sole, cut the pattern paper along the dotted line and add or subtract 1 cm for each size. Round off the new contour.)

from cotton fabric: 4 x sides cut along the fold, 2 x soles, incl. 1 cm seam allowance;

from fleece: 2 x sole, incl. 1 cm seam allowance;

from alcantara: 2 x soles, incl. 1 cm seam allowance;

from iron-on interfacing: 4 x sides, cut on the fold, 2 x soles, incl. 1 cm seam allowance

*1* Reinforce the cotton fabric and Alcantara (synthetic suede) pieces with the respective pieces of interfacing. Two of the side pieces form the outer part of the ballerina slippers. Make the little buttonholes, according to the pattern markings. First, sew around the buttonhole mark using a zigzag stitch, then carefully cut through the fabric along the marking. Next, sew up the seam down the rear centre of all side pieces, then press the seams open. Taking two side pieces, one with a buttonhole and one without, lay one on top of the other, right sides together, and sew together along the top edge, leaving a seam of 1 cm. Then, press flat, and stitch along the upper edge, leaving a 1-cm wide tunnel along the upper edge.

*2* With right sides together, sew the side piece to the Alcantara sole, paying special attention to front and back. Trim the seam back a little and iron.

*3* With right sides together, sew the fleece sole and the floral sole together, leaving a gap to turn. Trim back the seam allowance a little, turn the sole inside out and press.

*4* Glue this sole to the inner side of the Alcantara sole with adhesive. Then, sew the fleece sole to the seam allowance all the way round with a few hand stitches, closing up the opening in the process.

*5* Cut the velvet ribbon into four equal lengths. Cut the elastic into two equal lengths. Next, place one length of elastic between two velvet ribbons of equal length. With the seams lying flat on top of each other, sew together using a zigzag stitch.

6 Next, using a small safety pin, draw a ribbon through the tunnel of each slipper. Start at one of the buttonholes and gather the upper edge of the slipper as you go. When the ribbon emerges from the second buttonhole, make sure that it is evenly gathered all round, then tie the ribbon in a bow. Repeat this procedure for the second slipper

## Tip:

To keep your feet warm on cold winter days, you can use fleece rather than cotton fabric for the ballerina slippers. If you want to pep up the sleep mask, you can also decorate the mask with artificial eyelashes (available from most supermarkets and drugstores).

# Glossary

### Cutting out

When cutting out, always check the fabric grain is correct. With some fabrics you must also take note of the direction of the pattern or nap. Always leave sufficient space for the seam allowances between the pattern pieces. Avoid the selvedges. Measure the allowances carefully and draw them on with chalk before cutting out. Transfer all the important markings from the paper pattern to the fabric.

### Direction of pattern

If the fabric has a pattern that runs in one direction, all the pieces must be placed on it so that the upper and lower edges are pointing in the same direction. The "pattern" cannot be seen at first glance on all fabrics.

### Fabric

In the sewing instructions you will normally find recommendations for fabrics and quantities. However, if you want to choose an alternative fabric, it is advisable to decide beforehand whether you want to work with a firm or stretchy fabric. Working with firm fabrics is a little easier and more suitable for beginners. Stretch fabrics are not too difficult to work with. You just have to take care not to stretch the fabric too much when sewing, and use a special machine needle that is suitable for stretch fabrics. You must also use a stitch that leaves the seams slightly stretchy.

### Fusible interfacing

To make parts of the work firmer they should be strengthened with interfacing. Fusible interfacings (e.g. Vlieseline) are most commonly used, because they are very easy to work with.

### Grain of fabric

The warp threads of a woven fabric run parallel to the selvedge and constitute the grain. On patterns, the grain is indicated as a long straight line. If pieces are cut on a fold, this usually corresponds to the grain.

### Hem

The hem is the bottom edge of the article. First mark the length, then turn the hem allowance to the inside and pin or tack, press and trim to the correct width (rule of thumb: 4 cm). Then sew the hem by hand or machine. There is a difference between hems that are folded over once or twice. For hems with a single fold, the raw edges must be neatened before sewing the hem.

### Machine sewing

Seams etc. are always sewn by machine. If you don't have much experience of using a sewing machine, it is sensible to try out the various stitches, needle sizes etc. on a piece of old fabric first.

### Measuring

Before cutting out, always make sure you have the correct measurements for the piece to be cut out. Make a note of the measurements, if appropriate by transferring them to the paper pattern. Cut out the paper pattern, place it on the fabric, and transfer the measurements with tailor's chalk or pins. Then cut the fabric.

### Neatening

Raw edges must be neatened to prevent them from fraying. Seam allowances can be neatened before or after sewing the seam, depending on the pattern, and this is usually mentioned in the instructions. The easiest way to neaten seam and hem allowances is to use the zigzag stitch of your machine.

### Patterns

Large sheets of transparent tissue paper especially for this purpose are obtainable from specialist stores. Place the transparent paper on the pattern sheet and fasten in place. Then transfer all the lines and markings belonging to each piece.
Note: for some patterns the seam allowance is already

included in the pattern so does not need to be added when cutting out.

## Pressing

Iron all fabrics to remove the creases before cutting out, and press seams open when instructed. The iron temperature depends on the material. We recommend that you always use a steam iron.

## Right side

The right side is always the "front" side of a fabric. With patterned or structured fabrics the wrong and right sides are easily distinguished. With plain-coloured, woven fabrics you have to look more closely. When in doubt, the selvedge will help. This has small holes in it, which are always pieced through from the right side to the wrong side, so the smooth side of the holes is the right side.

## Right sides together

First place the right sides of the fabric – those that are later to be seen on the outside – lying against one another, pin in place and sew together on the wrong side.

## Seam allowance

Seam allowances of the same width make the job easier. When the edges of the fabric match, the sewing lines will automatically match too. Seam allowances must be taken into account when measuring and/or when producing a paper pattern.

## Sewing thread

Sewing threads are available in shops in different colours and qualities. They are suitable for hand or machine sewing. Choosing the right thread for a particular project depends on the fabric and what the seam requires.

## Tacking/pinning

Before a seam is sewn by machine, it should first be tacked or pinned. Place the pieces of fabric right sides together and pin together along the seam line or roughly sew together with tacking thread.

## Top-stitching

Top-stitching means you stitch along edges, hems or seams on the right side of the fabric to stabilise them and/or for decorative effect.

## Turning

Turning means that you sew two pieces together and then turn them right side out. Machine stitch the two pieces right sides together and trim the seam allowances to about 0.5 cm after sewing. With very thick fabrics, only trim one layer of the seam allowance, so the edge will lie more smoothly. Press the seams open. After turning the seam should lie exactly along the edge.

## Zigzag stitch

Zigzag stitch can be used to neaten edges by machine. It is very versatile and can be used to neaten both firm and stretchy fabrics. When using zigzag stitch in this way, make sure that the needle goes once into the fabric and once immediately next to the fabric edge. It is always best to try out the chosen thread and test the settings for the stitch width and length on a scrap of fabric.

## The authors

After studying fashion design, Rabea Rauer and Yvonne Reidelbach first worked for several fashion labels in the fields of design and pattern. Whilst working together as lecturers at a private fashion school, they soon came up with a plan to open a sewing café in Berlin-Friedrichshain. The "kinkibox" is a perfect venue for sewing hobbyists and would-be sewing fans to find all kinds of opportunities to give free rein to their creative instincts. Rabea Rauer and Yvonne Reidelbach are always on hand to offer advice and practical support – whether this means helping to put individual ideas into practice or organizing numerous sewing courses on themes which are currently in vogue. The kinkibox rooms with their charming attention to detail and comfy sofas and chairs provide the perfect atmosphere for a pleasant, post-sewing chat over coffee and biscuits.

www.kinkibox.de

## Acknowledgments

We would like to thank VSM Deutschland GmbH (Karlsruhe) for their help in producing this book.
www.singerdeutschland.de

## Please note:

## Picture credits

Photos: TLC Fotostudio (P. 26); Rabea Rauer and Yvonne Reidelbach (P. 47); Ullrich Alber (remaining photos); P.8/9: SINGER®/© 2013 KSIN Luxembourg II, S.ar.l.; Fotolia.com: © FreeSoulProduction (illustration of parcels), P. 30 © LeitnerR (cat)